2

Features

16

6

1

Mud Madness

What do you get when you mix lots of water and tons of dirt? Just add a thousand kids and you'll have Mud Day. It's the day when kids in one Michigan town get to play in a giant puddle of mud. Kids have wheelbarrow races in the muck, too. The muddiest boy and girl are crowned Mr. and Ms. Mud. Afterward, everyone gets sprayed clean with a fire hose.

In the Swim

A deserted island in the Bahamas is home to a whole herd of wild pigs. These pigs don't wallow in the mud. They live on a beautiful beach where they splash in the surf and nap in the sand. Don't worry. The pigs don't hog the beach. They are friendly and happily swim with people who visit the island.

More than Meets the Eye

Have you ever heard people say, "That's just the tip of the iceberg"? Most likely, they weren't talking about a giant piece of ice floating in the water. They probably meant that a problem was much bigger than it seemed. Icebergs are bigger than they seem. Only the tip of an iceberg sticks out of the water. Most of the iceberg is below the surface. Sometimes ships accidentally hit the part of an iceberg that is underwater because it is hard to see.

Rub-a-dub-dub

Do you like taking a bath? These monkeys do! They live in the mountains of Japan where it is snowy and cold. The monkeys have thick fur to keep them warm. Still, they like to warm up by taking a dip in hot springs. Hot springs are pools of naturally heated water. The water is heated by melted rock underground. When the monkeys are tired of taking a bath, they get out of the water and make snowballs for fun!

Body of Water

Every living thing on the planet needs water — especially you. In your lifetime, you will probably drink enough water to fill a swimming pool. Why will you drink so much water? Your body uses water for everything it does, even thinking. More than half of your body weight is water. Your brain is mostly water, and so is your blood. Your body gets water from the foods you eat and by drinking it. You lose water all day long by breathing, sweating, and going to the bathroom. To stay healthy, you need to keep putting water back into your body. So, drink up!

Make Way for Ducks!

Imagine how much fun it would be to have thousands of rubber ducks. They wouldn't fit in your tub. What would you do with them? You could have a rubber duck race. Many cities around the world hold rubber duck races every year. People pay money to put their name on the bottom of a rubber duck. Then the ducks are dropped into the river. The first duck to cross the finish line is the winner. The owner of the winning duck gets a prize. Later, the money that people paid for the ducks is given to charity. ★

Water, Water, Everywhere

Earth is called the "water planet." Looking at this photo of Earth, it's easy to see why.

In photos taken from space, our planet looks mostly blue. The large blue areas are oceans, which cover much of Earth. That's a lot of water, but it's not Earth's only water. The white areas in the photo are clouds and ice, which are also made of water. Even more water flows deep underground, where it can't be seen.

Earth is made mostly of water. Still, it is hard for many people to get the water they need for drinking, bathing, and cooking. Why? One reason is that very little of the water you see can be used by people. Most of it is ocean water, which is too salty to drink. It's also too salty to water gardens and farms where food is grown. Only a small amount of the water on Earth is salt-free, or fresh, water.

That leaves only a tiny amount of fresh water for drinking. This tiny amount of fresh water must be shared by everyone on Earth.

Only a Drop to Drink

If all of the planet's water were in one bucket, only a spoonful would be drinkable.★

The Never-Ending Story

The water that we drink has been on Earth since our planet was formed. New water never gets made. The same water just keeps moving around and getting recycled.

How does that happen? The sun warms water in oceans and lakes. Some of the water gets so hot that it turns to vapor. Most of the time, we can't see the vapor. The vapor rises into the air.

Snow

Water vapor moves through the sky as clouds or fog.

Fresh water turns to vapor with the sun's heat.

Rain

★ start here
Freshwater Lake

Water sinks deep into the soil.

When vapor cools, it forms little drops of water. Those tiny drops are what make steam, fog, and clouds. When the drops of water get large and heavy, they become rain. If the water drops freeze in the cold air, they turn to snow or hail. Drops of fallen rain and melted snow trickle deep into the ground or flow into rivers, lakes, and oceans.

Water in the ocean is salty. When salt water turns to vapor, the salt gets left behind in the ocean. That's why rain is never salty!

All of the water in the world has been going through this cycle for a long, long time. In fact, the water you drink today is the same water dinosaurs used to drink!

Drops of rain and melted snow run into rivers and lakes or the ground.

Freshwater Vapor

Freshwater River

When salt water turns to vapor, the salt gets left behind in the ocean.

Saltwater Ocean

How does water get to your faucet? Follow the blue pipes. First, water is pumped from lakes, rivers, or from deep in the ground into a water treatment plant. There, germs and other dirt are removed from the water so it is safe to drink. Then the water is pumped through pipes into a storage tank or tower. From there, water gets sent through pipes to your home and goes into the kitchen and bathroom.

 = Clean Water

= Dirty Water

Rain

Storage Tower

Lake

★ start here

Pumping Station

Underground Pipes

Water Treatment Plant

Where does the water go once you have used it? Follow the yellow pipes. When water goes down the drain or toilet, it goes into sewer (say it: SOO-er) pipes that are underground. The dirty water flows to a sewage (say it: SOO-ij) treatment plant. There, the water is cleaned. Then the water goes through more pipes into a river. And it finally flows back into lakes or oceans where the cycle starts all over again.★

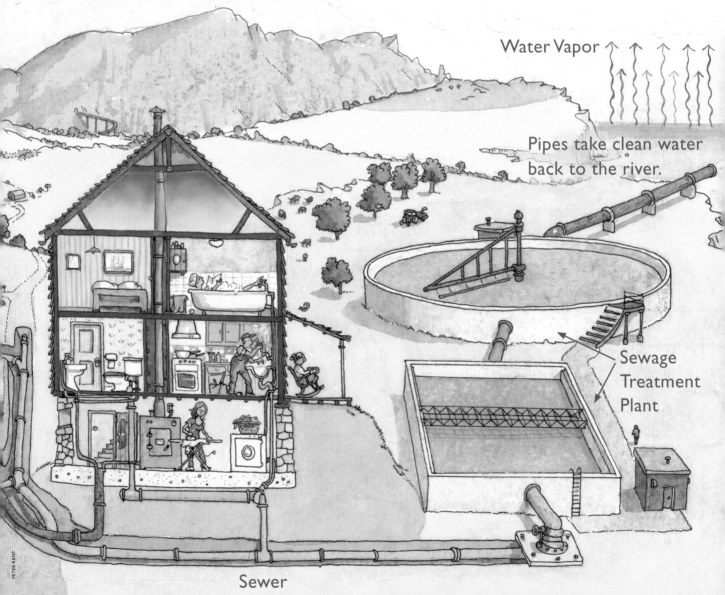

Water Vapor

Pipes take clean water back to the river.

Sewage Treatment Plant

Sewer

A Thirsty World

If you live in the United States, getting a cool drink of water is easy. It is usually as close as the drinking fountain in the hall or the faucet in your kitchen. But if you are a child living in many other parts of the world, getting a drink might be a whole day's work.

Many children in the world do not have fresh water piped to their homes. Their villages do not have the money to build water supply systems. Instead, they get water directly from ponds, streams, and other sources. Sometimes the water is dirty. Sometimes the water is far from their homes. Getting the water is often children's work because adults are busy working at jobs, cooking, or caring for babies.

Some children make many trips a day to get all the water their families need for drinking, cooking, and washing. Carrying water can take hours every day. It may leave no time for school or play. How do kids of the world get water?

Like many girls across the world, a girl in New Guinea (say it: GINN-ee) carries a water pot on her head. She walks miles to a place where it can be filled.

In the desert, a mother squeezes moisture from plants into her thirsty child's mouth.

A boy in Africa scoops water from a muddy pond. Dirty water can make people sick. But kids must drink it anyway when no clean water can be found.

Children in northern Russia (say it: RUSH-uh) gather snow to melt over a fire.

These girls in India dig for water in deep holes.

Luckily, people are coming up with ways for children to get water more easily. Also, new inventions help make water safer to drink. There is still much more work to be done, but these ideas are a great start!

Special straws can clean the water as children drink. Using the straws, these boys can sip clean water even from a muddy pond.

New rolling buckets let these girls bring home a day's worth of water in just one trip.

By pulling the handle on a pump, this girl in Thailand (say it: TYE-land) pulls water from a well deep underground. Water from underground is usually cleaner than water in lakes or rivers. And when new wells are built near schools, children can pump water at school and take it home after school.

There was no place to get water in this boy's village. Water had to be delivered by truck. It was very costly. It left families with almost no money for other needs. Then volunteers helped build a new well in the village. The well provides clean water at a very low cost. That's reason to celebrate! ★

15

Super Savers

It's important not to waste water. No matter where you live, fresh water supplies can run low. It happens when people use clean water faster than rain or melting snow can replace it.

You can help just by using less water. Even kids can make a difference! To start, try these simple steps:

Make sure the faucet is all the way off when you are finished using it. If you see a leaky faucet, tell an adult so it can be fixed.

Ask your parents to run the dishwasher or washing machine only when it's full.

Turn off the faucet while you are brushing your teeth. Turn it on again to rinse.

Take a short shower instead of a bath.

Use ice cubes to cool a glass of water instead of running the faucet until the water is cold. Or keep a pitcher of cold water in the refrigerator. ★

What makes popcorn POP?

If you've ever watched popcorn being made, you know that it must be very hot to pop. When hard corn kernels get super hot, they explode into a fluffy, white snack.

Most foods don't pop when they get hot. What makes popcorn special? The secret is water. A tiny bit of water is sealed inside every kernel. When the kernel becomes very hot, the water inside turns to steam. Steam takes up more space than water, so the steam begins pressing on the inside of the kernel's shell.

Soon, there's not enough space inside the shell for the steam. The steam breaks open the shell. Pop! Now the tasty white corn hidden inside the shell is on the outside. Sprinkle on some salt and dig in!

From Seed to Snack

Ears of corn grow on tall corn plants. Each ear is covered with hundreds of small, juicy seeds, or kernels.

The ears of corn are picked from the corn plant. Their leafy husks are removed. The ears are dried. A small amount of water stays trapped inside the kernels.

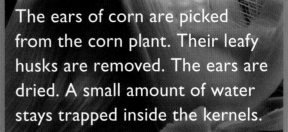

Cooking changes the kernels into a tasty snack. ★

The hard kernels are cut off the ear of corn and sold as popcorn.

ISTOCK

19

No Water? No Problem!

Camels live in the desert, where it's hot and dry. It hardly ever rains, and when it does, the water dries up very quickly. Even so, camels can make long trips in the heat and can go for a long time without food or water. How do they do it? Take a closer look at these amazing animals and find out!

One Hump or Two?

Some camels have two humps. Others have just one. Many people believe that a camel's humps store water. They don't. Humps store fat from the food camels eat. They also help keep camels cool. If the fat were stored all over their bodies, it would be like being covered in a thick padding. The fat would hold in heat like a heavy coat. Keeping fat in one place keeps camels cooler.

Lovely Lashes

As camels travel across the desert, hot winds blow sand around. The camels are well prepared. Their long eyelashes help protect their eyes from the sun and the sand.

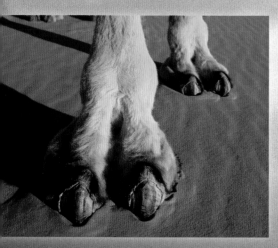

Hoof It

Some camels weigh 1,400 pounds. That's about as heavy as a whole class of second graders! Their hooves have special skin between the toes that spreads out as they walk. This skin keeps the heavy animals from sinking too far into the sand.

No Sweat

All living things need water to survive. In the desert, there is no water for miles and miles. Humans have to carry water with them. Camels don't. When a camel drinks, he really fills up. His body keeps that water inside as long as possible. Camels don't sweat like humans do. And when it's very dry out, camels don't lose much water when they go to the bathroom. Their noses can even catch the moisture from their breath and return it to their bodies!

Droopy Humps

As camels go for weeks in the desert without finding much food or water, their bodies use the fat in their humps for energy. This camel's humps have begun to droop. He needs to be fed. He also needs a big drink of water!

Ahhhhhh!

Camels travel for many months at a time. When they find an oasis (say it: oh-AY-sis) in the desert, they stop for fresh water. This camel is very thirsty. He drinks 25 gallons of water in less than 15 minutes! ★

Lost at Sea

Searching for Sunken Treasure

For hundreds of years, ships were the only way of moving cargo across the ocean. Ships sailed all around the world, often with loads of gold, silver, and jewels. But traveling through the ocean was risky. Hurricanes could strike without warning. Pirates or enemy ships could attack. Rocks, coral reefs, and even icebergs could poke holes in ships. If disaster struck, the ships sank, taking the treasure down with them.

Tons of treasure from these wrecked ships lies at the bottom of the ocean. Many explorers have searched for the lost treasure. Sometimes, they have struck gold! But the ocean is so big that treasure hunters may go for years without finding a thing. Turn the page to see some treasure that has been found—and some treasure that still waits for a lucky explorer to find it!

The Oldest Shipwreck

Who found it?

About 20 years ago, a diver saw some strange metal objects under the sea. A team went down to find out more. They found the ancient treasure!

What was on it?

The ship held gold and silver jewelry, bars of copper, and elephant tusks. It even held the world's oldest known book.

What happened?

Bad weather and rocky shores probably caused it to sink.

About the ship

A ship sank thousands of years ago near the country of Turkey. No one knows the name of the ship. It's one of the oldest shipwrecks ever found!

The Atocha

Who found it?

A determined diver and his team searched the ocean for 16 years before they found the treasure. It was worth millions!

What was on it?

There were gold and silver coins, chains, and bars. There were also lots of sparkling green emeralds.

What happened?

A hurricane hit, sending the ship crashing into the rocks near Florida.

About the ship

More than 350 years ago, the Atocha (say it: uh-TOH-chuh) was a Spanish treasure ship.

The Fleet of 11 Ships

Who found them?

A man started finding coins on the beach. Then he found one of the wrecked ships under the sea. He found seven more wrecks with treasure worth millions of dollars!

What was on the ships?

Lots of gold and silver was on board, including many valuable coins and emerald jewelry.

What happened?

A hurricane hit when they were off the coast of Florida.

About the ships

The ships were traveling to Spain almost 300 years ago.

The Hussar

Who found it?

Only the anchor has been found so far. The rest of the treasure is still buried under the muck and trash at the bottom of the river! Will it ever be uncovered? ★

What was on it?

Chests full of silver and gold.

What happened?

When it got to New York City, the ship struck a reef in the East River and sank.

About the ship

The Hussar (say it: hoo-ZAHR) sailed from England to the United States more than 200 years ago.

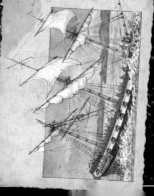

ISTOCK; JOHN RABOU, BILL CURTSINGER/NATIONAL GEOGRAPHIC STOCK; "MAX ALEXANDER/DK IMAGES; MEL FISHER'S TREASURES, ATOCHA TREASURE COMPANY LLC, WWW.ATOCHA1622.COM

Drip, Drop

What is fun to do on a rainy day? How can you make the best of wet weather?

The next time it rains, **invent your own milkshake.** Mix lots of flavors like strawberry, blueberry, cherry, and chocolate.

Sally, age 7

Go outside and **wash your dog in the rain.**

Tre, age 8

Hunt for earthworms. You can pick them up right off the sidewalk. You never see them lying around like that unless it's raining.

Hugh, age 8

Make boats out of paper or sticks

and race them in the water. It's fun!

Josie, age 8

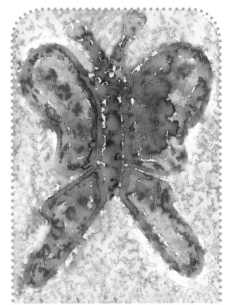

Paint with Rain

Watch raindrops turn your artwork into something magical! You'll need a stiff piece of paper and some washable markers. Draw a colorful picture. Then set the paper outside until the raindrops make the colors run. Bring your painting inside and let it dry. Now your masterpiece is totally transformed! ★

Play a **spy game.** Sneak around the house, staying low. Don't tell anyone where the best hiding spots are — that's classified information.

Coleman, age 9

Go outside and play. Ride your scooter and **jump in puddles.**

Bradley, age 8

A snack that will
make your mouth water

sea

A bowl

A spoon

Whipped cream
cheese

Blue food
coloring

A dinner plate

Mini bagels

A knife

Raisins

Fish-shaped
crackers

1 **IN** a bowl, mix half of the cream cheese with a few drops of food coloring. Spread the mixture on a plate. This will be the water for your sea monster.

2 **CUT** a mini bagel in half to make two half circles. Put one half aside. Cut the other half in two as shown above.

Monster

3 **PUT** the large half of the bagel cut-side down in the center of the plate. Place the smaller pieces of the bagel as shown.

4 **USE** dabs of cream cheese to stick two raisins on the head for eyes. Place crackers in the blue cream cheese.

5 **SHARE** your snack with your friends. Dip bagels into the cream cheese. Sea monsters are tasty! ★

Famous Falls

What makes Niagara Falls so fabulous?
Water, of course!

The thunder of rushing water grows louder. You shout with surprise as you get soaked with spray. Are you at a water park? No, you are aboard The Maid of the Mist, a boat that brings visitors  to Niagara (say it: nye-AG-ruh) Falls, the most famous waterfall in the world.

An amazing amount of water goes over Niagara Falls. The water that goes over the falls in just one second is enough to fill 25 swimming pools! When all of that water comes crashing down, it's a fantastic sight and a roaring noise.

LAKE SUPERIOR

WISCONSIN

LAKE MICHIGAN

LAKE HURON

MICHIGAN

LAKE ERIE

INDIANA

OHIO

ILLINOIS

Where does all the water come from?
The water that goes over Niagara Falls comes from four huge, connected lakes. After the water rushes over the falls, it flows into another large lake. Together, the five lakes are called the Great Lakes. There is more fresh water in the Great Lakes than in any other single place in the world, except for the ice that covers the North and South Poles.

The Great Lakes are fed by rain, melting snow, and spring water from deep underground. Every drop of rain and snow that falls around the Great Lakes will one day find its way into one of the lakes. Most of this water will one day go over Niagara Falls.

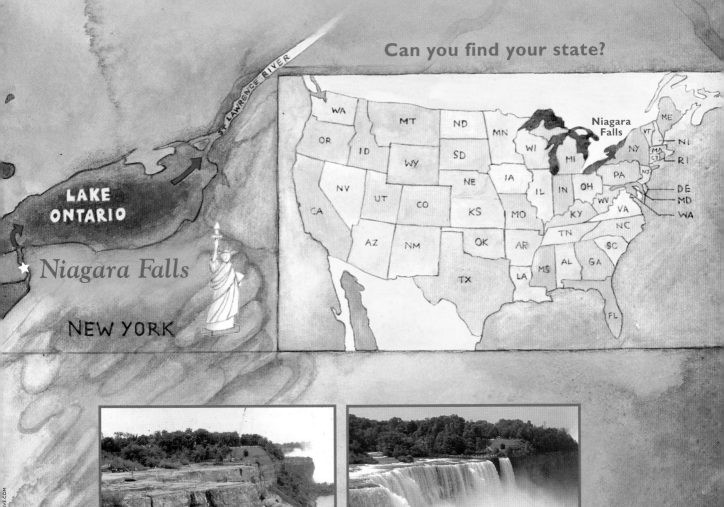

Can you find your state?

No-Water Falls

It's hard to believe these are two pictures of the same spot! In 1969, the rocks under Niagara Falls needed to be fixed. A dam was built to stop the water from flowing to one side of the falls. Imagine how strong that dam had to be to hold back all the water. ★

Then a lap around the world!

You have to lift a pickup truck over your head before the year ends.

I guess that's why they call it a pickup truck.

He makes you do pull-ups and chin-ups. Most kids do throw-ups.

Then you have to climb the rope. If you don't, he sets the bottom on fire.

They say there are still kids up in the ceiling.

But there are games, too. He makes you play dodge ball . . . with his truck!

And tag with Crazy Glue . . .

And baseball with real bats!

He makes you do handstands, headstands, nose stands, and music stands.

Uh, oh! There's his whistle! I better go line up.

I can't believe it! He's a regular guy!

Hi, kids. I'm Mr. Green.

Let's play basketball.

Score!

I'm going to like gym.

The End

OUCH!

Dear Ouch,
When I'm with new people I feel shy. I don't know what to say. How can I get over feeling shy?

Miss Mouse

If being with new people is hard, try making a game of it. Tell yourself you will find out five new things about one person. Ask questions! What does she like to do after school? What are her favorite books or movies? Does she have a pet? You get the idea. If you focus on other people, you won't have time to feel shy!

Dear Ouch,
Sometimes I'm late for school because I can't decide what to wear! What should I do?

Too Slow

Lay out your clothes before you go to bed. Think head to toe. Start by choosing your shirt and work your way down. Choose pants, socks, shoes, even underwear! Getting ready at night will make your mornings less rushed.

OUCH!

Dear Ouch,
My friends and I get in trouble for talking in class. I try not to, but it's soooooo tempting!
Wants to Whisper

Come up with a "stop" signal you can use with your friends when you have the urge to talk. You can make the zipped lips sign or just quietly tap your toes. If that doesn't help, ask your teacher if you and your friends can sit farther apart.

Dear Ouch,
Sometimes my mom is so busy that she doesn't answer my questions. How can I get her to pay more attention to me?
Ignored

Have you noticed that when a friend is playing a computer game it's hard to talk to them? Parents aren't that different from kids. If they are concentrating on one thing, they may stop noticing other things or people. Try saving your questions for a time when your mom isn't busy. If it's an important question, say, "Excuse me, Mom. Can you stop what you're doing for a second?" If you get someone's attention before you ask questions, you have a better chance of being heard. ★